Bibliographic information published by the German National Library:

The German National Library lists this publication in the National Bibliography; detailed bibliographic data are available on the Internet at http://dnb.dnb.de .

Imprint:

Copyright © 2014 GRIN Verlag, Open Publishing GmbH
Print and binding: Books on Demand GmbH, Norderstedt Germany
ISBN: 9783668218697

This book at GRIN:

http://www.grin.com/en/e-book/322764/the-relationship-between-memory-and-emotions-within-the-process-of-trauma

Timothy McGlinchey

The relationship between memory and emotions within the process of trauma and reconstruction

GRIN Publishing

GRIN - Your knowledge has value

Since its foundation in 1998, GRIN has specialized in publishing academic texts by students, college teachers and other academics as e-book and printed book. The website www.grin.com is an ideal platform for presenting term papers, final papers, scientific essays, dissertations and specialist books.

Visit us on the internet:

http://www.grin.com/

http://www.facebook.com/grincom

http://www.twitter.com/grin_com

Essay:

What is the relationship between memory and emotions?

The study of emotion is remarkably broad in its scope for anthropological concern, and the numerous influencing factors involved in it are invariably diverse. One factor that must not be underestimated is that of memory. It can be said that the two are interrelated through the influencing effect each has on the other, as will be expanded upon throughout this essay, as I dissect what I recognise as the most important elements of this memory-emotion connection. First, is the notion of "collective memory", and the influence of individual perception and identity within it. Also, I wish to examine the role of memory and emotion in the processes of trauma and reconstruction. In order to bring context to each of these areas, I will relate them to two main ethnographic case studies. The first is that of the maltreatment of Sudeten Germans and their displacement from Czechoslovakia, as researched by Svašek (2005). The second is a study by James (1997) who investigated fear in a transit camp for Sudanese asylum-seekers in South-West Ethiopia. Whilst focusing primarily on these, I will also make reference to Hinan's study of collective memory and reconciliation in Guatemala and Rwanda (2010). Throughout this essay, with reference to these studies and other relevant research, I intend to clearly outline the significant relationship between memory and emotions.

The first area I wish focus on is that of collective memory, which too lends itself to the notions of identity and individual perception. The link between these concepts is clearly demonstrated by Hinan, who says "memory shapes identity, memory establishes a collective narrative, and within that narrative, memory ascertains truth" (2010:20). To understand this statement fully, I wish to relate it to my first ethnographic case study of the Sudeten German expellees. During World War Two, most Sudeten Germans living in Czechoslovakia supported Hitler and the Nazi regime, which contributed strongly to already existing anti-German attitudes from the Czechs. At the end of the war, the Czech government ensured that the Sudeten Germans lost their citizenship and property, and so were expelled to Germany and Austria. However, during this time, many were killed by those who saw them as guilty of Nazi crimes. Svašek's research focuses on the traumatising consequences that arose through the displacement and violence towards them, and the emotional significance of their memories from this time. The effects of these events on the lives of the Sudeten Germans still persist today, as their identity has, to an extent, become shaped by their memories of their experiences. This link between memory and identity is a prevalent and reoccurring theme within this topic, and its significance is boldly described by Boyarin who claims that "identity and memory are virtually the same thing" (1994:23). The point Boyarin makes here is that the development of our identities is so dependent on the memories that shape it, the two could almost be seen as synonymous.

2

In more recent times, several organisations have been established which seek to recognise and appreciate the loss and oppression that the Sudeten expellees endured. It is through these, in part, that Svašek suggests an element of collective memory is established; "in some of these organizations, 'shared victimhood' forms the main raison d'etre". Svašek explains that this process of "shared victimhood" is linked to a concept known as "chosen trauma", coined by psychiatrist Vamik Volkan (1999) who sought to analyse the intergenerational transmission of trauma. Volkan argued that it is "more than a simple recollection; it is a shared mental representation of the event, which includes realistic information, fantasized expectations, intense feelings and defences against unacceptable thoughts" (1999:46). Moreover, it refers to a shared, adopted mind-set that acts as identification of a group, founded upon a traumatic event. The group does not *choose* to be traumatised, but they choose to install significance upon the incident; "what becomes important is the fact that the group carries the mental representation of the traumatic event" (Volkan, Berlin Meeting, 2004), the actual reality of the event loses importance. This concept is rooted in the emotional association applied to memories, but also the individual perception of memory, suggested through the term "fantasized expectations" (1999:46).

However, in recognising the individuality of memory, the reality of truth must too be questioned. As Hinan asserted, it is the formation of identity (from memory), and the consequent collective narrative that then leads to the truth. In recognising this subjectivity of "truth", Hamber and Wilson make the point that memory creates its own truth that may not be as accurate as historical truth (2002). Although, in a purely

3

technical sense this may be true, Nora's understanding of truth is that it is in fact more "truthful" than history, as it is the "truth of personal experience and individual memory" (2002:6). It is therefore the "truth", as exclusively understood by the expellees, as well as their shared victimhood or "chosen trauma", that forms their collective memory.

Another facet of this chosen trauma to which emotion is directly linked, is the "intergenerational transmission" that Volkan addresses. In the case of the Sudeten Germans, Svašek refers to "intergenerational projections of loss" (2005:203) as a way of explaining how it is not only the victims of terror who have been traumatised by the events after the war. Svašek demonstrates, specifically through the use of a poem written by an expellee, how attempts were made to "emotionally engage the next generation" (2005:204), not necessarily through the continuation of traumatic suffering, but instead through installing identity within the politics of shared victimhood. It was through a variety of mediums such as photographs, testimonies, shared belongings and others that this was achieved. This apparent intergenerational emotional inclusion is also addressed by Crumley when she says, "individuals pass on their behaviours and attitudes to others in various contexts but especially through emotional and practical ties and in relationships among generations" (2002:40). This once again reifies that importance of a memory-emotion interaction in the formation of collective, and indeed intergenerational, memory.

In many ways, this case study of the Sudeten expellees can be likened to Hinan's comparative study of collective memory in Guatemala and Rwanda. In her research,

4

Hinan describes both countries' post-conflict reparative strategies after the respective atrocities which occurred. She explains how in Guatemala, following the severe oppression and genocide that occurred in the country for nearly 25 years, those affected appealed for the "accretion of marginalised voices" (2009:21). Similar to the case of the expellees studied by Svašek, there was a shared recognition of victimhood within their collective memory. Testimonies were collected and even a theatrical project was organised to tell the stories of the oppressed entitled "There Is Nothing Concealed That Will Not Be Discovered". Sanford (2009), who recorded many of their experiences, said how the testimonies "portray the experience of the narrators as agents of collective memory and identity" (2009:21), and Hinan agrees that the memories they shared still had significant control over their actions. In this example of Guatemala, we can see the importance of emotions in the portrayal of memories, and in the subsequent shaping of identity.

This, however, is contrasted by what Hinan considers to be "failed memory" or "chosen amnesia" that resulted from the atrocities in Rwanda in 1994. In this case, the country had a "government-constructed narrative" which was formed under the assumption that forgetting the atrocities would be a more successful strategy than risking their persistence through free expression of victimhood. Therefore, their identity and collective memory was centred around the repression of emotion and memories, rather than their expression, as will be expanded on later.

This idea of post-conflict action, in fact, leads fluidly onto the next area I wish to examine which is trauma and reconstruction. To shed light onto this topic, especially that of trauma and fear, I will use the ethnographic case study conducted by James (1997), which focuses on the aspect of fear in a transit camp for Sudanese asylum-seekers in Ethiopia. The camp, called Karmi, was set up between 1992 and 1993 and was primarily occupied by Uduk and Nuer refugees. There had been a history of conflict between the two groups, especially directed towards the Uduk, and one of the most pertinent sections of the article focuses on one particular incidence of violence directed, instead, towards the Nuer. The Uduk, who had previously been part of a minority in Sudan, at this point in the camp, found themselves in a majority. James makes the point that the "epidemic of eager anger which carried the violence… was nevertheless the product of a longer history of feeling shaped by memories of fear and danger... Heightened emotion, drawing on memory at several levels, came to define these few hours of spontaneous violence" (1997:120). In relation to trauma, this quote is clearly suggestive of the importance of emotion and memory and the interplay between the two. The memories of subjection and fear for the Uduk which had accumulated for some time, revealed themselves through a display of violent emotion.

Collective memory, as suggested earlier, also contributes to the notion of trauma, as James says in reference to fear, it is "something anticipated, and thus pre-figured in the cultural imagination as it draws on collective memory" (1997:123). This explains why the actions of violence were not performed at a purely individual level but by a group – fear had become part of the Uduk's identity. As James explains, a "structure of feeling was in place, based on a more complex blend of short-term and long-term memories than might be evident on the surface" (1997:120). Although James' article is focused on the aspect of fear, it is frequently demonstrated throughout, like in the quote above, that the intricacies of it are rooted in the relationship between emotion and memory.

However, in considering trauma and fear, especially with reference to the case studies used, one cannot ignore the area of reconciliation. Most of the ethnographic examples used thus far have incorporated an element of reconstruction, but Hinan's study of Guatemala and Rwanda I see as particularly important in this discussion of memory and emotion. As she states; "(m)emory plays a crucial role in post-conflict reconstruction, as it aids the establishment of a collective memory, which in turn contributes to the creation of cultural identity, and the establishment of a narrative of truth, both of which are necessary in the rebuilding process" (2010:13). In the case of Guatemala, 80% of those either oppressed or killed were from the indigenous Maya population, and so through the process of establishing collective memory, they too embraced and reinforced their cultural identity. Manz (2002) remarked that through having their stories heard, they were also given an opportunity to grieve. Interestingly, in Svašek's study of the Sudeten expellees, grieving could also be recognised as a factor of collective memory and identity, because when referring to a commemoration for the lost lives of the Sudetens, she writes that "...the tears and handkerchiefs... produced feelings of communality" (2005:206). Fittingly, Ricoeur (1996) in fact refers to mourning as an act of reconciliation with loss, and acknowledgement of memory.

However, in the case of Rwanda, this "acknowledgement of memory" is starkly contrasted by the government-constructed "chosen amnesia". As the people of

7

Rwanda intentionally ignored the extreme conflict that occurred, they denied themselves the collective memory, and in a sense, the chance to maintain or develop cultural identity. As I hope I have already stressed throughout this essay, there is a strong, almost interdependent, link between identity and memory, and so through denying themselves the memory of the brutality that occurred, they tampered with their cultural identity, which Hinan states is "necessary in the rebuilding process" (2010:13). I believe the case put forth by Hinan clearly outlines the importance of emotion and memory in the process of reconciliation, whilst also incorporating other themes covered throughout, such as collective memory and identity.

In conclusion, having considered the various areas covered in this essay, I believe I have established a clear and undeniable relationship between memory and emotion. Firstly, in the ethnographic case study of the Sudeten expellees, the "chosen trauma" they experienced led to them forming a group identity that was fundamentally built on the severe emotional connections they established between their memories suffering and loss. These connections were also used in the process of "intergenerational transmission", whereby the identity shaped through these memories was in some way passed on to the following generation. Secondly, within the case study of the Sudanese asylum-seekers, it was clear that the persisting emotions carried on through their memories of fear, in some way, triggered their acts of violence. And finally through the comparative study of the atrocities in Guatemala and Rwanda, a clear need for the integration of memory and emotion was seen in the process of reconstruction, which resulted from the formation of collective memory and cultural identity. Therefore, it seems evident that a strong relationship exists between memory and emotion that infiltrates our perception of truth, our own personal and cultural identity, and even processes of peace and reconciliation.

Bibliography

Boyarin, J. 1994 *Remapping Memory: the Politics of Time Space*. Minneapolis: University of Minnesota Press

Crumley, C. 2002 Exploring Venues of Social Memory. *Social Memory and History: Anthropological Approaches* 39-53

Hamber, B and R.A Wilson 2002 Symbolic closure through memory, preparation and revenge in post-conflict societies. *Journal of Human Rights* 1, no. 1:35-53

Hinan, T. 2010 To Remember, or To Forget? Collective memory and reconciliation in Guatemala and Rwanda. *Totem: The University of Western Ontario Journal of Anthropology* 18, no. 1:13-22

James, W. 1997 The Names of Fear: Memory, History, and the Ethnography of Feeling Among Uduk Refugees. *The Journal of the Royal Anthropological Institute* 3, no. 1:115-131

Manz, B. 2002 Terror, Grief and Recovery: Genocidal trauma in a Mayan Village in Guatemala. In *Annihilating Difference, The anthropology of genocide* 292-309

Nora, P. 1989. Between Memory and History: Les Lieux de Mémoire. *Representations* 26:7-24

Ricoeur, Paul. 1999. Memory and Forgetting. In *Questioning Ethics: Contemporary debates in philosophy* 5-11

Sanford, Victoria. 2009. What is an Anthropology of Genocide? Reflections on Field Research with Maya Survivors in Guatemala. In *Genocide, Truth, Memory, and Representation*

Svasek, M. 2005. The Politics of Chosen Trauma: Expellee Memories, Emotions and Identities. In *Mixed Emotions: Anthropological Studies of Feeling* 195-214

Volkan, V. 1999 *Bloodlines: From Ethnic Pride to Ethnic Terrorism* Westview Press

Volkan, V. 2004 *Berlin Meeting*. http://vamikvolkan.com/Chosen-Trauma,-the-Political-Ideology-of-Entitlement-and-Violence.php

YOUR KNOWLEDGE HAS VALUE